Moving Beyond Belief

Moving Beyond Belief

A New Focus for the Christian Faith

RICK HERRICK

WIPF & STOCK · Eugene, Oregon

MOVING BEYOND BELIEF
A New Focus for the Christian Faith

Wipf & Stock
An Imprint of Wipf and Stock Publishers
199 W. 8th Ave., Suite 3
Eugene, OR 97401

www.wipfandstock.com

PAPERBACK ISBN: 978-1-6667-5209-0
HARDCOVER ISBN: 978-1-6667-5210-6
EBOOK ISBN: 978-1-6667-5211-3

10/07/22

For Charles, with deep appreciation

Contents

Acknowledgments | ix

Introduction | xiii

1   Jesus as Subatomic Particle | 1

2   The Bankruptcy of Belief | 10

3   A God of Love | 24

4   A Religion of Compassion | 37

5   Conclusion | 48

Bibliography | 57

Acknowledgments

MOVING BEYOND BELIEF HAS been a work in progress over the last fifty years. Despite this long-time span, there are only four people to acknowledge. The first is my wife. Lyn. She has encouraged me to pursue my passion for coming to an understanding of the riddles and mysteries contained within the New Testament when that search has without doubt negatively impacted my career success and ability to support our family. Her support has been a great gift.

The second is my old friend, Diane Dreher. I came to know Diane forty years ago when she was a regular contributor to a magazine I edited. Diane has had a distinguished career as an English professor, college administrator, and in her current position as associate director of the Applied Spirituality Institute at Santa Clara University. Among her many publications are three pathbreaking books on Taoism. Diane provided amazingly insightful criticism on the first two drafts of this book.

I met Tom Leach fifty years ago when we joined the faculty of a private high school in Jacksonville Florida. We were both finishing our dissertations. He taught in the English department, and I taught American history. In all the years I spent in the teaching profession, I never encountered a more gifted teacher. His enthusiasm for his subject, his empathy for students, and his breadth of knowledge are unmatched.

Tom left the high school three years before I did, and paved the way for my first university job. While I thank him for that, his help with my career was just the tip of the iceberg. He introduced me and guided me through the vast literature making up Eastern spiritual traditions. It's amazing I ever received tenure. His fascinating reading recommendations made it very difficult for me to focus on my research in Latin American politics. Thank you Tom for your friendship and inspiration over all these years.

Forty-five years ago, Lyn and I moved with our three children to a small town in North Carolina where I began my college teaching career at the University of North Carolina at Pembroke. I began as an assistant professor of political science. Our next-door neighbors were Susan and Charles Wentz.

About two months after moving there we invited the Wentzes for dinner. Not long after arriving, Charles walked over to examine some of the books in our library.

"I thought you are a political science professor?" he asked.

"I am."

"Then why all these books on religion?"

"Religion was my major in college," I responded.

"You're just the guy I'm looking for," he replied. "We need a Sunday school teacher for our young adults class. It will provide you with an opportunity to meet some of the finest people in our town."

Charles was the Sunday school superintendent for the local Presbyterian church.

Because I have a hard time saying no, I accepted his offer. It changed my life. I was soon spending more time preparing for the Sunday school class than my classes at the university.

But Charles has done far more for me than getting me started on my lifelong journey of searching for the historical Jesus. He has been both a loyal and an inspirational friend. He inspires me because there are few people I know who do a better job living the love the New Testament is all about. From the perspective of this book, this guy knows God in a deep, experiential sense. It is therefore my great honor to dedicate this book to him.

Finally, I would like to thank again the Wipf and Stock staff for their friendly cooperation in putting this project together and for their considerable help with editing the final draft. I have worked with five publishing houses, and this group is in a league of their own.

Introduction

THIS BOOK IS ABOUT the misplaced focus of many Christians on religious belief. As a result, it is appropriate to begin with my favorite story about belief which comes from Russia. It takes place in the tenth century. It's about how Russians adopted the Orthodox faith. It is particularly relevant at this time because it helps to explain the current disaster of Russia's invasion of Ukraine.

Grand Prince Vladimir 1 was a pagan with a consuming ambition to unify the Russian tribes into a single nation. He considered several possible approaches to integrating the state, and eventually decided the best way to achieve his goal was to use religion.

He sent out special emissaries to explore three possibilities. The first was Roman Catholicism. Although there were no doctrinal issues that concerned him, he concluded it would be dangerous to subject his country to the political intrigues and power struggles of Western Europe. He also looked into Islam, and rejected it for similar reasons. Actually, this process of deliberation was more pretense than real because conversion to the Greek Orthodox faith would enable him to marry the beautiful sister of the Emperor of Constantinople whom he coveted.

Introduction

In 988, Vladimir forced all ethnic Russians to be baptized into the Orthodox faith at sword-point along the banks of the Dnieper River. One man's lust decided the religious fate of an entire nation. Over the years Russian Orthodox Christians came to believe that only they practiced religion in a manner acceptable to God. This claim is a remarkable one considering the fact these people could have become Muslims if the Muslim ruler during Vladimir's search had had a beautiful daughter.

If the truth is known, we are all like those Russians tribes. I am an Episcopalian because my father lusted for a beautiful Episcopalian, my mother. If one were to reroll the cosmic dice, that woman of my father's dreams could have been Mormon or Seventh Day Adventist. The consequences for me would have been different childhood stories. Such stories become embedded in the complex electrical systems of our brain, and develop into the background music that defines our lives.

Religious belief is acquired when young children are "brainwashed" with all good intentions by loving parents. Religious belief survives because some people desire unambiguous and comforting answers to the complex and sometimes tragic problems that confront them. Christian religious belief survives because some people fear death and crave an eternal life with Jesus. Religious belief survives because it often solves character defects such as alcoholism, anger management, or drug addiction.

An important truth to note about religious belief is that it is a human creation. While many religious traditions claim their beliefs come from God, the evidence presented in Chapter 1 will make clear that Christian belief has come from human minds and not the mind of God. Genuine revelation, the encounter of divine love, has no connection to religious belief. Religious belief is like all ideologies. It is a system of ideas created by human beings to answer questions deemed to be important. Revelation from God has no content. It is about a heart that is overflowing with love.

Why write a book whose central purpose is to criticize the fact that for most Christians the focus of their religion is centered around belief? The answer is quite simple. They are missing the point. The truth about religion has nothing to do with what you believe, but rather has everything to do with a heart that overflows with divine love.

This problem of focus has significant consequences. Christians whose religion is defined by correct belief, whose religion is an ideology that does not touch their heart, have little interest in and no ability to live the teachings of Jesus. Their chief concern is personal salvation. Because they believe Jesus provides that salvation, they worship him; but they do not follow him. They do not make a concerted effort to live by his teachings and the example he set with his life. Chapter 2 presents overwhelming evidence in support of this conclusion.

As Chapters 3 and 4 make clear, to pattern your life after Jesus requires a new heart, a heart that overflows with the love and sense of goodness that comes from God. That new heart creates a perspective that is enlarged, a way of seeing the world that goes beyond self-centered concerns. It enables a Christian to live the vision of Jesus, a vision defined by a deep concern for economic and social justice, inclusion, and the practice of nonviolence. Chapter 3 presents several practical suggestions on how such a new heart is acquired.

There has never been a time when living the vision of Jesus has been more important. The survival of our planet requires real solutions to the problems of climate change and the ever-increasing threat posed by the spread of nuclear weapons. Our democracy is threatened by a lack of civility among the partisan players, most of whom claim to be Christian. The fact that they can't get along strongly suggests their religion is defined by belief and not a full heart that comes from knowing God. Gun violence in our country is out of control, and the economy has never been more skewed in favor of the rich.

For thousands of years religions centered around belief have exacerbated social and political problems like those listed above. They have fueled conflict between nations. The Christian religion is no exception to this rule. It is time for us as Christians to change the focus of our religion from personal salvation to living the vision of Jesus. Jesus dedicated his life to bringing God's kingdom of love to Israel. If we want to be followers of Jesus that needs to be our mission too.

A few explanatory notes are necessary before we get started. I will use traditional notations for Jewish and Christian scriptures because I find the terms Old Testament and New Testament more specific and less likely to lead to confusion. By adopting this strategy, I do not imply in any way that Christian scripture represents a higher form of revelation than Jewish scripture. The texts from both religions were written by human beings with their own challenges, problems, and special stories of inspiration. I will, however, use CE for common era which replaces AD and BCE for before the common era, a replacement for BC.

Fifty-five years ago I purchased my first Bible, *The Jerusalem Bible*, for a New Testament class I was taking in college. Our professor chose this Bible because it was written in plain English and because it came with introductions for each book and explanatory notes scattered throughout. The gospel references cited in this book come from *The Jerusalem Bible*.

Finally, you will quickly notice biblical references follow many of the points made in the book. It is important for you to check these references especially if you come across something you don't understand or have difficulty agreeing with. To check the scriptural reference against the point I am making will greatly enhance its impact. Because I know most of you won't do that, I'm going to make an offer. I will pay anyone one hundred dollars if they discover a passage I have misused or misrepresented.

I make this offer because I want readers to have confidence in the passages I cite, but there are two qualifications. First, I will only pay the first person who discovers a problem. I can't afford someone ganging up on me and telling all their friends, "Hey let's get this guy." I will send a picture of a cancelled check to all those who respond too late. Second, if I can show the point I am making conforms with mainline biblical scholarship, I will write a letter listing authors that support my position which will not include a check. Please email me at rherrick86@gmail.com with questions or any problems you discover. I look forward to hearing from you.

1

Jesus as Subatomic Particle

I HAVE BEEN HOOKED on the study of the historical Jesus for the past fifty years. The most honest characterization of this Jesus I have come across in all of my reading comes from John Dominic Crossan. Crossan compares Jesus to a subatomic particle. Physicists employ the strongest microscopes in their laboratories to try to locate the parts of the atom, but they are too tiny for them to see. They escape all positive identification. It is only possible to know these particles by the effect they exert on the particles around them.

Like a subatomic particle, Jesus is best known by his effect. The truth is that history can't find the historical Jesus as I will point out below. On the other hand, the resurrection produced a profound effect. The followers of Jesus were left with a deep sense of his living presence. The problem is that it is very difficult to translate this sense of presence into historical details regarding his life, which helps to explain why history can't find him.

An even better explanation is found in the Roman/Jewish War from 66–73 CE. Palestine during the time of Jesus was a Roman colony. There was widespread discontent as a result of burdensome Roman taxes and threats to Jewish culture. While the Galilee of Jesus was relatively calm during his lifetime under the rule of Herod Antipas, the situation rapidly deteriorated from 40–66 CE, which led to direct Roman rule to stem the chaos. In 66, Jewish freedom fighters seized the Roman fortress at Masada, and then proceeded to throw the Romans out of Jerusalem. Rome eventually counterattacked with 60,000 troops, one soldier for every Jew living in the city. In 70, Roman troops entered Jerusalem, burned the entire city to the ground, and destroyed the temple. Mass crucifixions ensued, with tens of thousands of Jews killed. Many others were enslaved. A few lucky ones were able to flee. Jerusalem ceased to exist as a city. It became a ghost town. The Jesus movement was forced to move from Jerusalem to the Hellenistic world.

Prior to that move, there was a well-organized Jesus movement in Jerusalem under James, Jesus' brother, that came into existence soon after the crucifixion. These followers obviously collected and wrote down stories about Jesus. Sadly, these stories were lost. If gospels were written in Palestine before 70, they have never been found. Eyewitnesses were killed. The only historical data we have from first-century Palestine concerning Jesus comes from the oral tradition, stories passed down about him by word of mouth. To make things more difficult, these stories had to make the transition from Palestine to the Hellenistic world. The First Gospel, Mark, was written forty years after his death.

The quest to discover the Jesus of history began 250 years ago. Since the eighteenth century, three such scholarly quests have taken place. Each new quest has been accompanied by new historical methods and techniques, and each quest has ended in more confusion. Scholars agree that Jesus was a first-century Jew from Galilee, that his parents were named Mary and Joseph, that he taught in parables, and that he was crucified in Jerusalem. But that's it. Because the Gospels differ so widely on the details of Jesus' life, ministry, and mission, scholars are all over the map on these issues. Let's spend time with some of the problems.

Does a story go back to Jesus? The Gospels feature miracle stories throughout. Conservative scholars present good arguments these stories are based on credible historical memory.[1] More liberal scholars make equally good arguments these stories are works of fiction.[2] What is one to believe? What about a saying of Jesus? Does it accurately report the words of Jesus? Scholarly opinion differs widely on this question as it pertains to a particular saying and reflects a similar division noted above for stories.

It is widely known that the evangelists felt no qualms about putting words in Jesus' mouth, which indicates this problem of whether a saying goes back to Jesus is more than one of memory. There are many examples of this practice with perhaps the clearest one being Jesus' dying words on the cross.

> My God, my God, why have you deserted me. (Mark 15:34; Matt 27:47)

> Father, into your hands I commit my spirit. (Luke 22:46)

> It is accomplished. (John 19:30)

The above quotations represent three different sayings regarding Jesus' last words on the cross. Two of these sayings must have come from evangelists and not the historical Jesus. It is likely all three sayings were invented by the evangelist and the words placed in the mouth of Jesus.

Though this problem is seen throughout the Four Gospels, it is most evident in John. Read the Gospel of John and you will see that it consists, for the most part, of many long speeches made by Jesus to a single person or his disciples. There is no evidence that the person Jesus spoke to was taking notes, and the disciples were known as illiterate peasants. There were no recording devices in the first century, which leads to the question of the authenticity of the speeches. You can't remember speeches of that length word for word. Many scholars have argued that, in fact, the speeches were

---

1. A representative sample of scholars in this camp include: N. T. Wright, Josh McDowell, R. T. France, and Lee Strobel.

2. A representative sample of scholars in this camp include: Robert Funk, Marcus Borg, John Shelby Spong, John Dominic Crossan, and Bart Ehrman.

sermons by first-century Christian prophets which the evangelist placed into the mouth of Jesus.[3]

Scholars who focus their study on the Jesus of history, the Jesus prior to the crucifixion, see him differently. Some picture him as a Jewish mystic,[4] others as a Cynic-like peasant in the tradition of Roman Cynic philosophers,[5] and still others as an eschatological prophet, a prophet concerned with the "end times" of history.[6] These differences are not insignificant and point to the real problem of achieving a consensus regarding who the Jesus of history really was.

Scholars differ on key questions that pertain to Jesus' life: Why did Jesus go to Jerusalem? Did he anticipate his death? Did he see himself as a prophet? Did he see himself as more than a prophet? What does the title "Son of Man" designate? Was there a trial? Was Jesus buried?[7]

This last question is interesting, because if Jesus was not buried and was left on the cross to die (most victims of Roman crucifixions were left on a cross to be devoured by animals), then a physical resurrection would not have been possible. There would have been no body to resurrect. The New Testament is clever in that it documents both possibilities. The Four Gospels present a physical resurrection, a position that assumes a burial. Paul, the first to write about the resurrection, portrays it as a vision experience. He has a vision of Jesus alive in heaven (Acts 9:1–9). He also insists quite adamantly that his encounter of the resurrected Jesus was the same as that of the disciples (1 Cor 15: 4–8).

> But get up and stand on your feet, for I have appeared to you for this reason: to appoint you as my servant and as witness of this vision in which you have seen me. (Acts 26:16)

3. An excellent discussion of these issues can be found in Anderson, *Riddles of the Fourth Gospel*.

4. Borg, *Meeting Jesus Again*.

5. Crossan, *Historical Jesus*.

6. Allison, *Historical Christ*; Ehrman, *Jesus;* and Fredriksen, *Jesus of Nazareth*.

7. Allison, *Historical Christ*; Ehrman, *Jesus;* and Fredriksen, *Jesus of Nazareth*.

Was the resurrection of Jesus a physical event or a vision experience? The difference between these two possibilities is quite significant. A literal reading of the New Testament provides for both possibilities. Again, what is one to believe? Let's go back a step and look at the meaning of Jesus' death on the cross. This is a key event for many Christians. For the writer of the Gospel of John, Jesus' death was seen as an atoning sacrifice. Jesus, for John, was the perfect sacrifice, the lamb of God who takes away the sins of the world. Jesus died on the cross for our sins, which is what most Christians like to believe.

The Gospel of Luke places no such significance on Jesus' death. Luke portrays the historical Jesus as Israel's last prophet. As Jesus dies, the earth is covered in darkness, a symbol of prophetic judgment. (Luke 23:44) There is no hint in Luke that the death of Jesus has anything to do with sin.

My preferred explanation for the significance behind Jesus' death comes from Mark. According to Mark, the experience of innocent suffering leads one to God. The Roman centurion provides the clue. As Jesus suffers on the cross, the Roman centurion, as a witness to the event, declares: "In truth, this man was a Son of God" (Mark 15:39).

As Jesus dies in Mark's account, the veil of the temple is torn from top to bottom. Jews believed that God resided in the temple in a room called the holy of holies. Because God was regarded as so sacred, the presence of God was hidden by this veil. The only person allowed in that room was the high priest, and only once a year when he performed an atonement ritual on behalf of the people of Israel during the Yom Kippur celebration. Mark is telling us all that changed with Jesus' death. Now, through a deep experience of the suffering surrounding Jesus' death on the cross, all people would receive access to God. The monopoly of the high priest was broken. Again, like Luke, there is no hint in Mark that Jesus' death had anything to do with sin.

What is one to believe? A literal reading of the Gospels presents three distinct views.

Let's look at the important question of salvation. Where is the kingdom of God located? Where will salvation take place? Stephen, the first Christian martyr, has a vision of Jesus in heaven at the right hand of God. Salvation is in heaven (Acts 7:55–56). Paul has a similar view (see Acts 9:1–9; 1 Thess 4:13–18):

> At the signal given by the voice of the Archangel and the trumpet of God, the Lord himself will come down from heaven; those who have died in Christ will be the first to rise, and only after that shall we who remain alive be taken up in the clouds to meet the Lord in the air. (1 Thess 4:16–17)

Jesus prays to his Father in heaven (the famous Lord's Prayer) that God's kingdom comes to earth as it is in heaven. While heaven is the model, the location is earth (Matt 6: 9–10). In addition, Jesus promises his disciples they will sit on thrones to judge the twelve tribes of Israel:

> You are the men who have stood by me faithfully in my trials; and now I confer a kingdom on you, just as my Father conferred one on me: you will eat and drink at my table in my kingdom and you will sit on thrones to judge the twelve tribes of Israel. (Luke 22:28–30)

There is a little confusion as to who will be the citizens of the kingdom: the people of Israel or all the peoples of the world. Jesus states two positions on this issue, as is reported in Matthew. It is obvious one of those positions does not come from him. Someone from the early church was putting words in his mouth, most likely the idea that the kingdom would be for all of the world's people.

> Do not make your way to Gentile territory, and do not enter any Samaritan town; go instead to the lost sheep of the House of Israel. (Matt 10:5–6; see also Matt 15:24)

> Go, therefore, make disciples of all the nations; baptize them in the name of the Father, and of the Son and of the Holy Spirit. (Matt 28:19)

As the two examples above indicate, there is confusion as to where the saved will reside and who will be the new residents of God's kingdom.

How does one gain entrance to the kingdom? Was one saved by grace, an undeserved gift from God as reported by Paul, or did one have to earn admission by doing good works, the position of Jesus? A careful reading of the Sermon on the Mount (Matt 5–7) makes Jesus' position on works quite clear. The contrast in views between Jesus and Paul is documented in the following passages:

> No; that faith is what counts, since, as we see it, a person is justified by faith and not by doing what the law tells him to do. (Rom 3:28; see also Rom 4:13–16 and 11:5–6)

> For the Son of Man is going to come in the glory of his Father with his angels, and he will reward each one according to his behavior. (Matt 16:27)

On one question as it relates to salvation, the New Testament is crystal clear. These events, the "end times," were seen as imminent. God's kingdom would arrive within the first century.

> I tell you truly, there are some standing here who will not taste death before they see the kingdom of God. (Luke 9:27)

In my book on evangelical Christianity,[8] I did a study on this issue. I listed every reference to the coming of God's kingdom in the New Testament. There are more than 100 passages that speak to this question. In not one of those passages was there a suggestion there might be an extended delay. Every reference indicated the kingdom of God was imminent. Many of these claims, like the one in Luke above, were made by Jesus. There is only one conclusion one can draw from this. Jesus was wrong, and this was not a mistake over a minor issue.

The analysis above covers some of the most important issues in the New Testament, but I've only scratched the surface when it comes to the confusion surrounding the historical Jesus. Was

8. Herrick, *Case against Evangelical Christianity.*

he the pre-existent Son of God, with God from the beginning of time, as portrayed in the prologue of John (1:1–18)? Or was he a human being who became the Son of God at his baptism by John the Baptist at the start of his ministry (Mark 1:9–11)? Did the ministry of Jesus last for one year (the Gospel of Mark) or did it take place over a three-year period (the Gospel of John)? Did the cleansing of the temple occur at the end of Jesus' ministry (Mark 11:15–19) or at the beginning (John 2:13–20)? Did Jesus counsel his followers to refrain from the use of violence (Matt 5:21–22) or did he counsel them to take up the sword (Matt 10:34)?

What about the books that didn't make the official New Testament Canon? Gnosticism was a prominent Christian movement in the second and third centuries. Fifty-two gnostic texts were found in a cave in Egypt in 1945. Gnosticism combined the teachings of Jesus with Eastern traditions. Jesus brought salvation by bringing mystical, direct knowledge of God to his followers. He was seen as a divine being who came to earth to lead his followers back to the light, a symbol for the divine presence of God.

Gnostic beliefs about Jesus were quite different from the picture of him in the Four Gospels that make up the canon. As the institutional church gained in authority, gnostic beliefs were declared to be heretical. When Constantine made Christianity the official religion of Rome in the early fourth century, he ordered all heretical books burned. There were many of them, which tells us that early Christianity had a wide variety of views with regard to the historical and the postresurrection Jesus.

Here's the point of all this. If the Christian faith is about belief in Jesus, what is a person to believe? If one is honest about it, an objective assessment is not possible. There is no reliable historical data upon which to anchor belief. This problem does not bother many Christians, however. Why? Because they invent their own Jesus by carefully selecting the facts about him in the New Testament that suit their needs and wishes. They then ignore passages in Scripture that do not support their picture. The Bible as the literal word of God seems only to apply to passages that support their preconceived ideas. As a result, their religion is a human invention which the next chapter will demonstrate has not worked out that well.

2

The Bankruptcy of Belief

THERE IS A MUCH greater indictment of the Christian religion as belief than the confusion described in the last chapter. Toward the end of his famous Sermon on the Mount, Jesus sets a standard for determining true religion: "You will be able to tell them by their fruits" (Matt 7:16–20). True religion is defined not in terms of correct belief but in terms of actions. Does a person act in terms of his own narrow self-interest or does he act to benefit others? A brief review of the history of the Christian church over the last 2,000 years will demonstrate a very poor record when it comes to carrying out the vision of Jesus.[1] The church as a collective entity has not been the bearer of good fruit throughout much of its history. To repeat what I said in the introduction, Christians prefer to worship Jesus than to do the hard work of trying to live their lives according to his teachings.

We'll begin with what some have called the Jesus wars, wars fought primarily among Christians in the name of the Prince of

1. Over the years I have consulted many books on the history of the Christian church. There are some differences between them, but on most issues they are quite similar. One of the best is: MacCulloch, *Christianity*.

Peace over issues of religious belief. The first of these wars came about in the aftermath of the Council of Chalcedon in 451.

Early Christians had a hard time resolving the problem of Jesus' nature. Some Christians focused on divinity, arguing that Jesus had one divine nature, that he was fully divine. They were called Monophysites. Arians focused on a more human Jesus. The group that eventually won, Chalcedonians, joined the two natures into one person. Jesus was defined as fully human/fully divine. Each group argued their formula was absolute truth and essential for salvation. Belief in the wrong formula would send you to hell.

This Chalcedonian solution came about as a result of historical chance. The Monophysites, those believing in a fully divine Jesus, were the dominant group in the Roman Empire for most of the first six centuries of Christian history. Two historical accidents led to their defeat.

In 449, at the Second Council of Ephesus, the Monophysites gained a decisive advantage. A vicious doctrinal cleansing took place. Church councils were not quiet, dignified affairs in which bishops sat together waiting for the spirit of God to descend and tell them what to believe. Instead, they were political brawls. At Ephesus, two-nature bishops were forced to return home, armed thugs beat up dissenters, and votes were influenced by bribery and threats. Council participants engaged in name-calling, slander, and intimidation.

Just as the Monophysites gained clear ascendancy, Emperor Theodosius II, a key supporter of the Monophysite position and an organizer of Ephesus, fell off his horse and died. He had no heirs. In the immediate aftermath following his death, Theodosius's sister, Pulcheria, became the power behind the throne. As a two-nature fanatic, Pulcheria organized the Council of Chalcedon, which met in 451 to put the church's stamp on the two-nature doctrine of fully human/fully divine. Had Theodosius not fallen from his horse, there would have been no Chalcedon. Jesus would have been forever defined as a divine being, as God on earth. His human side would have been seen as heretical.

Sadly, this did not end the dispute. The two sides fought for the next 200 years. Because state power was weak during those days and unable to control private violence, armies loyal to bishops were given free reign. Tens of thousands of Christians were killed in what historian Philip Jenkins has labeled the Jesus Wars.[2] These Christians were fighting among themselves over issues of religious belief, all in the name of the Prince of Peace who taught them to love their enemies and to pray for those who persecuted them.

This disastrous split over church doctrine weakened Christian unity and made it possible for Islam to spread into formerly Christian lands in the late seventh and early eighth centuries. A series of popes provided an answer to this problem. The First Crusade was launched in 1074, followed by the Second Crusade in 1147. Both were holy wars fought to stop the advance of Islam. The Third Crusade, launched in 1201, began as a war against Islam and was later directed against Eastern Orthodox Christians centered in Constantinople. Popes promised their soldiers salvation in heaven for their participation in these wars to defend the faith. Such a promise has a creepy, modern ring to it.

Martin Luther really stirred things up when he sent his Ninety-five Theses to the Archbishop of Mainz on October 31, 1517. The immediate issue concerning his protest was the sale of indulgences, a practice the Catholic Church used to raise money with the promise that it would lead to the forgiveness of sin. Luther argued that only faith in Jesus Christ would lead to such forgiveness. The larger issue was over church authority. The Roman Catholic establishment claimed that authority must be centered in the church as an institution, while Luther and his followers placed authority solely in the Bible.

By 1525, large areas of Europe were in flames over these issues of belief. Luther praised the violent defense of his ideas. Fighting between Protestant and Catholic princes over these issues raged off and on for over 100 years. The wars ended with the Peace of Westphalia in 1648, a treaty that allowed each prince to determine the religion of his state. In the process, historians have estimated

2. Jenkins, *Jesus Wars*.

that between 25 to 50 percent of the populations of Germany and France lost their lives fighting over church doctrine.[3]

Moving to the modern period, Rwanda received her independence from Belgium on July 1, 1962. Rwanda is populated for the most part by two ethnic groups—the Hutus and the Tutsis—both of whom are Christian. Since independence, the majority Hutu have had a history of killing Tutsis. Events spiraled out of control on April 6, 1994, when President Juvénal Habyarimana's airplane was shot down. Hutus went on a rampage and, over a three-month period, 800,000 Tutsis were slaughtered.[4] The horrifying thing is that Roman Catholic and Protestant churches for the most part stood aside and allowed this genocide to unfold. It was a common occurrence for Hutus to slaughter their brothers and sisters in Christ in places of refuge like schools and churches.[5]

A similar genocide involving Christian groups occurred within the former Yugoslavia. The breakup of the Soviet empire in Eastern Europe in 1991 led to a similar breakup within Yugoslavia. Ethnic nationalism led to the establishment of independent republics in Serbia, Slovenia, Croatia, Bosnia, Herzegovina, and Macedonia. This led to the Yugoslav Wars from 1991 to 2001. These wars involved a series of separate but related ethnic conflicts with causes deeply rooted in the history of the area.

The Bosnian War took place in Bosnia and Herzegovina between 1992 and 1995. To simplify things greatly, the conflict was between the armies of the Republika Srpskaand the Republic of Bosnia and Herzegovina. The Republika Srpska was Serbian, and their citizens were predominantly Greek Orthodox Christians. The Republic of Bosnia and Herzegovina was largely Croatian, and their residents were Roman Catholics.

Serbs and Croats have a long history of conflict in that area, with much of it resulting from their religious differences. The

---

3. For a good discussion of the devastating consequences of the Thirty Years' War, see MacCulloch, *Christianity*, 644–47.

4. History.com Editors, "Rwandan Genocide," para. 1.

5. "The Rwandan Genocide," *Holocaust Encyclopedia*, United States Holocaust Memorial Museum, Washington, DC.

Bosnian War was characterized by bitter fighting, indiscriminate bombing of villages and cities, ethnic cleansing, and mass rape. These atrocities were mostly perpetrated by Serbians, but Croat and Bosnian forces were also involved. The war ended when NATO intervened in 1995 and launched airstrikes against the army of the Republika Srpska, forcing the Serbs to sue for peace.

As I type these sentences, Russia is invading Ukraine. A few days prior to Russia's invasion, Russian President Vladimir Putin gave a dark speech in which he claimed Ukraine was an indispensable part of Russian history, culture, and spiritual heritage. Two days later, Patriarch Krill, the head of the Russian Orthodox Church, blessed both Putin and the troops as they prepared to invade. He praised Putin's leadership as a miracle of God, and framed the invasion as a larger metaphysical struggle against immoral Western values. This invasion, which has led to several charges of Russian war crimes, is an attack of Russian Orthodox Christians against their Orthodox brothers and sisters in Ukraine.[6] Christian nationalism is unfortunately a widespread problem that infects congregations the world over.

To review briefly, the wars described above were conducted by Christians, most often involving questions of church doctrine. In many cases, the participants believed they were fighting to honor the Prince of Peace, whom they claimed was the central focus of their lives. As I will point out in chapters 3 and 4, these wars would not have taken place if these participants had known God rather than merely believed in him. Stay tuned.

The long history of anti-Semitism in Europe paints an equally dismal picture. It didn't begin that way as we see with the first followers of Jesus under his brother James in Jerusalem. These early followers remained in the synagogue as a Jewish sect. It didn't take long for that to change, however. The problem began with the evangelists spinning the passion narrative in such a way as to make

---

6. Thames, "Putin Is After More than Land." In all fairness, as the brutality of Russia's invasion became more apparent, 280 Orthodox priests issued a statement condemning the attack. It is important to note, however, that these priests represent only a small minority of priests within the Russian Orthodox church.

the Jews responsible for Jesus' death. The goal was for Christians to escape Roman persecution by convincing Roman authorities that Christians were harmless, that Pilate was not responsible for the death of Jesus, and that Rome had nothing to fear from this new religion. It is difficult to take Rome off the hook, however, because crucifixion was a Roman punishment.[7] If the Jews had wanted to kill Jesus, stoning was their method.

A brief overview of European history is informative. The First Crusade (1096) was directed against both Muslims and Jews. The cry went out that the Jews had crucified Christ, which led to their being threatened with conversion or death.

It became a common practice for European Christians to blame Jews for all the tragic events that occurred in their lives. The Black Plague (1348–51) took the lives of between 20 and 25 million people. Jews were accused of causing it, which led to thousands being randomly killed in revenge. Roman Catholics blamed the Jews for the Reformation. Both Catholics and Protestants blamed the Jews for the revolutions in Europe of 1830, 1848, and 1871.

The aftermath of the Black Plague led to hysterical anti-Semitism in Spain. In 1391, Jews were ordered to convert to Christianity or face the death penalty. This harsh discrimination was institutionalized in 1478 when King Ferdinand and Queen Isabella established the Spanish Inquisition. This religious tribunal was designed to enforce Catholic orthodoxy. Organizers were especially suspicious of the forced conversions of Muslims and Jews. Were the conversions for real or merely faked to avoid punishment? Many converts were accused of being dangerous heretics. Over the 300 years of the tribunal's history, 150,000 people were prosecuted and between 3,000 and 5,000 executed.[8] The religious frenzy led to mass expulsions of Jews and Muslims from Spain.

The Dreyfus Affair showed that anti-Semitism existed just below the surface in French society. An army officer and French patriot named Alfred Dreyfus, who also happened to be Jewish, was arrested and charged with spying for the Germans. He was

7. Carroll, *Constantine's Sword.*
8. Carroll, *Constantine's Sword,* 357.

convicted on these bogus charges in December 1894 and sent to prison. The charges of a Jew spying for the Germans led to a massive explosion of anti-Semitism in France.

One of the biggest anti-Semites in Europe was Martin Luther. For that reason, Hitler loved him. It is interesting that Pius XII, the pope during the Nazi period, strongly condemned Communism but remained silent in the face of Nazi atrocities. When Hitler demanded German church leaders sign loyalty oaths and accept his racial policies, the vast majority of German clerics went along in silence. The one prominent exception was Dietrich Bonhoeffer. Bonhoeffer was quick to point out that silence in the face of evil is evil itself; to not act is to act. Bonhoeffer lost his life fighting the anti-Jewish policy of the Nazis.[9]

The Christian church has a long, sad history of remaining silent in the face of discrimination. Churches in the Southern United States have long supported slavery, even after the Civil War. Martin Luther King expected white churches in the North to be his biggest supporters. Most remained silent. The Dutch Reformed Church in South Africa has a long history in support of apartheid. Such Christians believe in an ideology, but have never known God's love in a deep, experiential sense. Such love naturally reaches out to those who are different.

Moving to a problem which has only become manifest in modern times, there is no greater long-term threat to the health of our planet than human-induced climate change. The place to begin is with the science that explains the problem. There is a broad consensus among scientists that global warming is occurring because of human activity. The basic science is simple to understand. The burning of fossil fuels has increased the level of carbon dioxide in the atmosphere by 40 percent since the beginning of the industrial age. This carbon dioxide acts like a blanket by refusing to allow heat to escape from the atmosphere. The result is global temperature rise. During the twentieth century global surface temperatures have increased by $1.33°$ F. Computer models suggest that by 2100 the global surface temperature will

9. Metaxas, *Bonhoeffer*.

rise an additional 2.0° F at minimum, with a maximum possible gain of 11.5° F.[10]

Global warming is causing glaciers to melt, leading sea levels around the world to rise. This increased heat adds moisture to the atmosphere and increases the energy in the climate system, which incites extreme weather. Increased levels of carbon dioxide have also found their way into the oceans, which changes the chemistry of the water, thus posing a significant long-term threat to several species of aquatic life. Significant expenditures now to contain this global scourge will pay dividends for the future because out-of-control global warming will have enormous negative economic consequences.

As I suggest above, the consensus on these conclusions is virtually unanimous within the scientific community. Opinion polls tell us that people around the world are largely in agreement with the scientists. The picture in the United States is not quite so clear, however. Conservative Christians by large majorities reject these scientific conclusions.

Climate change-deniers argue that only God can cause global temperatures to rise. If the planet is warming, humans have nothing to do with it. Senator James Inhofe (R-OK), the chair of the Senate Environment and Public Works Committee, holds that view. According to Representative Paul Brown (R-GA), "God's word is true, but evolution, embryology, and the Big Bang Theory are lies straight from the pit of Hell."[11]

These men believe the world was created by God in six days and is 9,000 years old. Forty-six percent of Americans believe in the literal version of the two creation stories in Genesis. A similar number attribute the increased intensity of storms and flooding as evidence of the biblical end times. Their bedrock commitment to the literal truth of Scripture prevents them from seeing that in fact there are two stories of creation in the first three chapters of Genesis with no common elements between them. Read the first three chapters of Genesis and list the events of creation for each

10. Bushby, "Why Climate Change Matters More," 49–57.
11. Flannery and Werline, *Bible in Political Debate*, 61.

story. You will quickly see that the order of creation is different for each story and that the two stories have little in common.

You can't be in love with God without being in love with the created universe. Climate change threatens the health of God's creation as well as the quality of life of our children and grandchildren. As I listened to the political debate pertaining to the Congressional elections in November of 2018, the climate change issue was rarely discussed. The real danger is that there is no forgiveness with this issue. Greenhouse gases emitted into the atmosphere today will remain there for thousands of years. Christians need to stand up and join together in demanding a responsible solution to this problem. God is tugging at us to do so. There really is a better way to provide energy to fuel modern economies than a heavy reliance on fossil fuels.

The other problem that threatens the planet with destruction is the prospect of nuclear war. During the Cold War years, the United States and the Soviet Union built nuclear bombs. By 1986, the US arsenal included 23,000 such bombs, with the Soviet arsenal reaching 40,000. Each of these bombs was, at minimum, several times more powerful than the nuclear bomb that destroyed Hiroshima in 1945. The yield of some of the larger bombs was 1,000 times more powerful than the ones used at the end of World War II. The national security policies of the two states were insane, morally bankrupt. An all-out war between the two countries would have ended human life on the planet. And we came so close![12]

US government officials during the Cold War claimed we needed such an arsenal to deter the Soviet Union. These claims by government officials were untrue. Such deterrence is achieved when a country can survive a nuclear strike and retaliate with devastating consequences. Nuclear deterrence can be achieved with one Trident II submarine, which has enough nuclear firepower to totally destroy twenty-four Russian cities. Trident II submarines can hide in the ocean and remain virtually invulnerable to Russian attack.

The United States's nuclear arsenal was designed for war fighting. Our weaponry was organized in such a way as to decapitate

12. Ellsberg, *Doomsday Machine*, 144.

the Soviet Union with a first strike. Such a strategy meant attacking Soviet command and control centers as well as their missile silos and air bases. In launching the attack, enough weapons were to be held in reserve to threaten Soviet cities if they fought back. There are three horrible problems with this strategy. First, the Soviets might have responded with a launch on warning. The arsenals on both sides were on hair-trigger alert. The simple misreading of a radar screen could lead to a nuclear strike. Second, submarine commanders and those commanding missile sites the US failed to destroy could have calculated that their country was destroyed already and retaliate in anger. The result of these first two problems is general war with the end of human life on the planet.

The third problem points to the immorality of a warfighting strategy. Such an attack would kill hundreds of millions of people living in Russia, Europe, and China from the blasts themselves, from firestorms resulting from the blasts, and from radiation fallout. Most of the dead would be innocent civilians. I don't know how any sane person could pull the trigger on such an attack. Reflect and pray about such a situation. What is God's messaging, the inner voice emanating from your heart, telling you?

Nuclear warfighting was planned to be used to protect Europe from a Soviet invasion. Very soon after the invasion, US policy was to counterattack with nuclear weapons. This policy remains in place. The reason for the policy is to save money. Deploying sufficient troops to deter a Soviet attack was deemed to be too expensive. The problem with such an approach is that it places the lives of millions of innocent Europeans at risk, which makes the warfighting strategy morally bankrupt.

Use of nuclear weapons was threatened against North Korea and China in 1953 in an attempt to end the Korean War. A similar threat was made against China in 1958 in the Quemoy and Matsu crisis, two islands claimed by Taiwan which China threatened to occupy. First use was also threatened against the Soviet Union during the Berlin crisis in 1961, and by Nixon during the Vietnam war. The world was lucky nobody called our bluff.

In a fascinating book entitled *The Doomsday Machine*, Daniel Ellsberg points out another scary problem.[13] The idea that only the president can decide to use nuclear weapons is a myth. Beginning with the Eisenhower administration, theater commanders were given the right to initiate the use of nuclear weapons under certain conditions. This policy was put in place to guarantee deterrence in the event Washington was destroyed and theater commanders were unable to receive a presidential order.

The Soviet Union also had such a policy which came close to producing Armageddon during the Cuban Missile Crisis in 1962. The Kennedy administration quarantined Cuban waters to prevent further missile-related equipment from the Soviet Union reaching the Island. The administration warned the Soviet Union that their four submarines would have to leave the area. An official explained to Moscow that American destroyers would drop hand grenades into the water to signal the subs to surface. The four Soviet submarines never received that message. Upon hearing the exploding hand grenades, one sub commander believed he was under attack and that the war had started. Because he was unable to communicate with Moscow, he and the other officer holding the nuclear keys wanted to attack with a nuclear armed torpedo to defend the honor of the Soviet navy. By chance the squadron commander was on board holding a third key, and he refused. That refusal to initiate a nuclear strike saved the world.

Since the end of the Cold War some rationality has returned to this madness. The START 1 treaty, signed by the United States and Russia on July 31, 1991 set a limit of 6,000 nuclear warheads for each side with a limit of 1,600 ICBMs and bombers. The treaty reduced the number of operational strategic warheads by 80 percent. The New START treaty entered into force on February 5, 2011 following Senate ratification. This treaty limits the number of deployed launchers (ICBM, submarine, and bombers) to 700. A total of 1,550 nuclear warheads can be deployed on these launchers.

Amazingly Henry Kissinger, George Schultz, William Perry, and Sam Nunn, all prominent members of our national security

13. Ellsberg, *Doomsday Machine*.

elite, called for much deeper cuts and the eventual establishment of a nuclear weapons-free world. In contrast, President Trump recently called for a 1 trillion-dollar investment in modernizing our nuclear force over a ten-year period. His administration will try to sell this reckless policy as important for deterrence, but it's really about warfighting. Remember: one Trident II submarine is all that is necessary for deterrence, and we have fourteen of them. I mention the Trump plan only to suggest that convincing our national security elite and the US Congress to dismantle or even to reduce further our nuclear arsenal will not be easy.

Make no mistake about it, however. The scourge of nuclear war is a Christian issue. It is in fact the paramount right-to-life issue of our time. Christian groups from around the globe must come together and demand that their governments take action to create a nuclear weapons-free world. Sadly, as with so many other issues discussed in this chapter, Christians have for the most part remained silent. I can only conclude that their silence results from a religion defined by correct belief. Only a heart that overflows with God's love will convince you that this nuclear madness must end.

I want to end this chapter with a discussion of the Prosperity Gospel because in a strange way it sets the stage for the discussion that follows in chapters 3 and 4. The Prosperity Gospel has its roots in the Protestantism that grew out of the Reformation, with values such as thrift, delayed gratification, and hard work as the path to gain salvation. The fact that one was rich proved you lived those values and that God was on your side.

The Prosperity Gospel first came into prominence in America in the 1950s. It teaches that God rewards faith with wealth and good health. Jesus is pictured as a staunch supporter of individual responsibility and limited government regulation. Poverty is a sign you have sinned. The message of pastors from such churches is to have you think that a gift to the church is an investment. Your investment will only multiply to your benefit. The goal of life is to amass wealth. A *Time Magazine* poll in 2006 found that 17 percent of American Christians identified with the movement.[14]

14. Van Biema and Chu, "Does God Want You to Be Rich?," 2.

Even the most cursory reading of the New Testament suggests that this approach to religion is contrary to the teachings of Jesus, the guy who proclaimed the last would be first, that the rich man would have trouble entering the kingdom of God, and that to be his follower one should first give all their possessions to the poor. Matthew 19 speaks to all three teachings, but these sentiments are found throughout the Four Gospels.

In the next chapter, I'm going to argue that one's religion reflects one's personality structure. Many Prosperity Gospelers seem to possess a weak ego, a personality structure distorted by fear, a sense of grievance, envy, with an inner emptiness that creates an insatiable appetite for things. They feel like they somehow haven't measured up, from which comes a sense of shame. They develop a deep sense of grievance with the thought that society has somehow cheated them. As a result, they see riches as solving their problems by proving their critics wrong. Wealth and Jesus are their saviors. Wealth tells them that God loves them and proves their self-worth. Jesus takes them to heaven. It's a perspective that distorts the message of Jesus. It's a perspective that prevents them from knowing God in a deep, experiential sense as you will see in the next chapter.

As the examples from this chapter illustrate, a religion of belief does a poor job producing fruits that relate to the vision of Jesus. For many of these Christians it is easier to worship Jesus than to live according to his teachings. I left out many issues that provide additional support for this claim. The church has a long history in support of patriarchy. Self-righteous missionary activity in the nineteenth century destabilized societies in the Third World and among Native Americans in this country. That same spirit of self-righteousness is responsible for the idea of American exceptionalism which has poisoned our relations with other countries in the world. We are a Christian nation that prefers to feed the military rather than the poor. We are a Christian nation whose energy consumption and lust for unlimited economic growth threatens environmental collapse. We are a Christian nation where the level of economic inequality is one of the worst in the developed world.

I'm going to argue in chapter 4 that the problems outlined above violate the vision of Jesus. This sad situation exists because most Christians practice a religion of belief rather than a religion that comes from knowing God. A religion of belief is an ideology which can provide meaning for the follower. The problem with religion as an ideology is that it doesn't touch the heart. Yes, there are exceptions, but not enough so that the Christian religion can become a part of the solution to the world's problems rather than a cause of those problems. Thus, the time has come for us to shift our focus.

3

A God of Love

WE BEGAN THE LAST chapter with the standard Jesus set for determining true religion: that you will know them by their fruits. Christians who participate in wars over belief, who discriminate against those who are different, who deny the science documenting climate change, who remain silent with regard to the threat posed by nuclear weapons, and/or who fall for the false prophets selling the Prosperity Gospel do not pass that test. The problem is they have never known God. What does it mean to know God?

God is met in an encounter of deep love. You sense from this experience that you are at one with the universe, that life is good and beautiful, and that love is built into the structure of the universe. It's a love that wants to reach out to others who are in need or who are different.

The experience tells you the whole is so much greater than the sum of the parts. This encounter is an experience that can't be defined or explained. God is not some concept that can be believed. Instead, we encounter God in a profound, intimate experience that is often deep enough to rearrange one's personality.

This encounter takes place in the soul, the place where humans and God meet.[1] You sense this meeting place lies within, but the soul's location remains a mystery. Martin Buber, for one, argues that we meet God in the social space between two individuals who are relating to each other with a sense of empathy and concern.[2]

The soul generates thoughts that float through our awareness, reflecting God's goodness and love. The problem is the human ego generates thoughts of a different sort that reflect a person's self-centered concerns, thoughts that are organized around survival, thoughts that stem from the oldest structure of our brain dating back to our reptilian past. These ego-derived thoughts compete with the thoughts of God from the soul and drown out the sense of goodness and love that comes from God.

The ego is a personality structure organized around our insecurities and demons. It's based on the assumption that we need to be defended, that we are separated, isolated, and in need of protection. In pursuit of our defense, the ego generates thoughts that tell us to win, to succeed, to compete. Ego-generated thoughts condemn others and seek revenge when it believes we have been attacked. The ego attempts to control others as a means of self-defense. It creates thoughts that we are under attack so that we will pay attention to it. These self-centered thoughts function as a dense smokescreen that block the thoughts of divine love emanating from the soul.

The good news is that God wants to be known and that there are ways to penetrate the ego's smokescreen. Once you do you quickly learn that the ego's self-centered perspective is not the real you, that you do not need the ego's protection.

The apostle Paul had his egocentric smokescreen blown away on the Damascus Road.[3] He was on a trip to further his efforts to

---

1. The theoretical discussion of the spiritual aspects of personality was helped along by Rohr, *What the Mystics Know;* Fox, *One River, Many Wells;* Naranjo and Ornstein, *On the Psychology of Meditation;* and Corbett, *Religious Function of the Psyche.*

2. Buber, *I and Thou.*

3. Borg and Crossan, *First Paul* and Armstrong, *St. Paul.*

persecute the followers of Jesus. As he was traveling into the city, he suddenly encountered a light from heaven. The experience was so powerful he fell to the ground, and then he heard the voice of Jesus asking him why he continued to persecute his followers. The experience lifted the scales from Paul's eyes, and he saw the world differently (Acts 9:18–19). His personality was transformed.

The essence of the spiritual journey is to see ourselves and the world differently. As I will point out in the next chapter, that new perspective leads to a passionate concern for economic and social justice as well as a commitment to nonviolence. The prophets had a similar transformation. Walter Brueggemann argues that the central role of the prophets was to imagine alternative futures. They came to see the world in a new way.[4]

Returning to Paul, despite the fact that he had worked so diligently to persecute the followers of Jesus, his encounter made clear that God still loved him—deeply. This realization created an experience of divine love that was so intense it transformed him as a person (Acts 9:3–9). His belief system was overwhelmed by the encounter. He had been a champion of the temple, a strict adherent of the law. The idea of a crucified Messiah was scandalous. All that changed when the smoke was cleared away. The smokescreen was lifted in such a way that he was able to live the rest of his life as a soul-centered person. He became a prophet of divine love.

Many of the Old Testament prophets received similar encounters of deep love which transformed them. You can read about Amos's visions in chapters 7–9 in the book under his name. Isaiah was called by God in 742 BCE. His inaugural vision shows him overwhelmed by God's love and goodness (Isa 6:1–13). Jeremiah received a similar encounter in 627 BCE (Jer 1:4–19). Finally, Ezekiel had several visions of God's deep love and mystery (Ezek 8–11).

Unlike the prophets, Jesus is harder to document because the Gospels never report an inaugural experience. The Gospels do, however, provide us with some hints. They report that he spent forty days in the desert facing his demons, which he defeated (Matt 4:1–11). When demons are found to be part of a false self the ego

4. Brueggemann, *Prophetic Imagination*.

has created and you reject them as not representative of your best self, the smokescreen is lifted and love floods your awareness.

Some of the short, often enigmatic, aphorisms for which Jesus was so famous hint at such an approach to religion. In Luke 6: 45, he claims that good people draw what is good from the store of goodness in their hearts. He ends a brief parable on choosing your place at the table by commenting that everyone who tries to preserve his life will lose it while anyone who lets go of life will find it. (Luke 17:33) Again in Luke, (14:11) Jesus states that anyone who raises himself up (is ego driven) will be humbled in contrast to the one who humbles himself. He will be raised up.

Jesus is also portrayed as a God-infused person. He sees God everywhere—in a mustard seed, in the lilies of the field, in the table fellowship he shares with an array of interesting characters. His teachings clearly emanate from his soul, which we will explore in the next chapter. The evidence above suggests that Jesus knew God from deep encounters he received during his lifetime.

I end with my own example because it illustrates a different process of coming to know God. Unlike Paul and the prophets, I have not received a profound inaugural vision. My coming to know God has been a long, two-steps-forward-one-step-back journey. Though the process was different, the end result of the journey has been the same.

Before delving into the techniques that have guided my journey, let me make a brief comment about gurus. The Buddha taught that each person must find his or her own path. No gurus or teachers were needed. I have followed that advice, but it may not be the best advice for all people. Many spiritual seekers have found teachers to be very helpful. There is probably no right answer to this issue. My preference, as I indicate above, has been to proceed on my own. That suits my personality, but I may have made faster progress with a good teacher.

Moving on to a discussion of my journey, listening to music uncovers my soul. I love to hike, and there have been times when the beauty of nature has blown me away. Witnessing the suffering of another clears away the smoke.

Thirty years ago I spent two weeks with my parents while my father was dying. It was an especially difficult time for me because my Dad was only sixty-nine. He seemed so young, and I was a long way from being finished with him.

His problem was congestive heart failure, and he was at home on oxygen with a heart that was having trouble functioning. Two days before he died I was in the living room with my mother talking about the people to call to report on my father's failing condition. The calls were my job.

For some reason Dad decided to walk from their bedroom into the living room, dragging the portable oxygen machine behind him. I was amazed he was able to make the trip on his own, and I am in tears today as I type up the experience of watching him make that effort. My mother immediately left the couch where we were sitting, and they met in the middle of the room.

It was their last dance. Dad had come to say goodbye to my mother. He told her how much he loved her, that marrying her was the best decision he had ever made. It really did look like they were dancing, with my mother holding him closely to provide stability while they relived some of the sacred times in their marriage.

I remained transfixed, sitting on the couch. At some point during this final dance, this special couple became encased in light. Love was radiating throughout the room. You could sense it, feel it, almost touch it. My heart was so filled with love it was bursting. My Dad, who I loved deeply, was dying, and yet the world looked so beautiful. Reflecting on the experience later, I was convinced I had been in the presence of God.

I have had two similar experiences. The first of these occurred when I witnessed the birth of our daughter Molly. It was an encounter triggered from a sense of awe and wonder as this precious bundle appeared on the scene. The hospital room was flooded with goodness and love.

Three years later, after a late night of grading papers, I decided to check on our son before going to bed. I entered his room. It was hot, with the fan unable for the most part to relieve the heat, and his diaper was soaked. As I gazed at him asleep in his crib, my heart was flooded with love. The room became brighter. Life was really good, special, and I left with a new name for God. I named God More Than. The reality of that experience was so much greater than what was literally present in that room.[5]

But here's the thing. These special experiences weren't transforming. The smoke cleared, but it eventually came back. I learned that God can be known from the experiences described above, my listening to music and hiking in beautiful settings, and it encouraged me to begin reading the literature on Eastern spiritual traditions and the Christian mystical tradition. But I was still the same Rick.

What I learned from my study was that inner work was required to make the sense of God's presence a more permanent fixture in my life. The good news is that there are many approaches to mystical union with the divine, an approach suitable for every personality. The bad news is that this work, at least for me, has not been easy. It's been a long journey, a journey that has required disciplined practice, but one should not be discouraged by this. Modest gains are continually made along the way. You seem to make progress in plateau-like stages.

Over the years I have looked for and experimented with different techniques to remove the smokescreen on a more permanent basis. I eventually settled on a technique called contemplation.[6] In silence, I sit, close my eyes, and examine my life. I look at my insecurities, what motivates me, what causes anger, the people who bother me, situations that cause anxiety. The search is conducted objectively without judgment. My goal is to understand what lies behind this darkness and then to reject it as not representative of my best self. Aspects of my personality, like a perceived need to control others or to have all the answers, I have come to understand are not the real me. They're part of an invented self that seeks to protect me, but with time I have learned I don't need that kind

5. For a wonderful discussion of God as the great More Than, see Frantz, *God You Didn't Know.*

6. Rohr, *What the Mystics Know.* Three additional books that have been helpful are Burklo, *Mindful Christianity;* Naranjo and Ornstein, *On the Psychology of Meditation*; and Underhill, *Practical Mysticism.*

of protection. When you look your demons directly in the face and refuse to identify with them, they lose their power. The smoke lifts.

I supplement the above practice with two additional meditations. The first is a meditation on the goodness in people. I begin seated in silence, watching my breathing as a means of quieting my overactive mind. Once that is achieved, I focus on people I know. The purpose is to look for the God within them, to look beyond the masks they wear and the roles they play to find the goodness within.

Have you ever wondered about divine wisdom, what it is and where it comes from? I did until I started meditating. When I work on a person I'm having trouble with, in silence and at peace, the most creative thoughts on how to deal with the situation come into my head. It's wonderful! Sophia,[7] the female face of God, the face of wisdom and creativity, is speaking to me.

Finally, I meditate on gratitude. After a quiet mind is achieved, I thank God for all the blessings in my life. I also reflect on the miracle of my existence, on how the billions of cells within me know just what to do. Then there is the fact that my body conducts 100,000 different chemical reactions without my knowing it. Amazing, God. You're good! This is my favorite meditation because I always leave with an overflowing heart.

In an important sense, meditation is about what your awareness seizes upon. There is so much out there to choose from. Left on their own, humans tend to process what is out there with a false, created self, a mindset that places them at the center of the universe. Meditation is about attaining a wider spectrum of awareness. As you move beyond an egocentric perspective, you see the world differently. The smoke clears. You discover a love that wants to reach out to others.

I have a good friend who once described God as the conductor of a symphony orchestra. Before performing, the musicians tune their instruments so they can play in harmony while following the conductor's lead. I meditate as a way of tuning up. It enables me to hear God's gentle prompting of goodness and love.

7. Sophia is a well-known designation for the wisdom of God.

One of the most encouraging things about this approach to religion is that, in addition to those profiled above, all of the great spiritual leaders in world history practice a form of it.[8] According to the Buddha, religious doctrine is a human invention that gets in the way of truth. God is not an idea to believe, but a reality to know. Enlightenment is about cleaning the windows of perception. It is about getting rid of egocentric attachments that encase the soul. With clean windows, love shines through. The key to right living is to let that love rule your life. The Buddha could have written this book.

Lao Tzu taught that the Tao can't be defined, only known through an experience of oneness and deep inner peace. The Tao is described as a pattern of infinite beauty and goodness that flows in and around us. It becomes known by aligning yourself with the patterns of nature. To experience nature in that way humbles us. It puts our ego in its place. The smoke encasing the soul is lifted.

The Bhagavad Gita is contained as a small part of a much larger Hindu poem. A vision of God as radiant beauty shines throughout. On a literal level, the poem describes a battle between two families. Many have argued that the story is a metaphor for purifying the soul—a battle to extinguish desire and egocentric attachments. Once the smoke has cleared, Brahman, the god of love, beauty, and goodness, shines through.

Several years ago I had a persistent dream about the world's great spiritual traditions. I would drive to the base of a mountain, park the car, and walk around. On that walk I encountered several missionary types urging me to climb the mountain along their path. Some claimed their path was the shortest way to the top, a few claimed their path was the only way. After traveling along several paths, what I learned was that each one led to the summit above the tree line, a place of wonder, beauty, deep peace, love, and goodness. With regard to religious experience, all traditions are one.

Let me end this chapter by making two points about religious belief. The first point is that there is a difference between belief as a means and belief as an end. I have a friend who believes Jesus

---

8. Fox, *Christian Mystics*.

died for him on the cross with the result that his sins are now forgiven. When he reflects on Jesus' suffering on his behalf, he is overwhelmed by a sense of gratitude and love. His reflection on this belief punctures the smokescreen encasing his soul. It makes no difference whether this belief is historically true. What is important is that his reflection on Jesus' suffering was the means by which he came to know God.

Belief as an end so often becomes an ideology with no connection to the heart. The notion that I am saved by correct belief does nothing to clear away the smoke. An exclusive focus on salvation in heaven is all about me and works to increase the smoke. The idea that my religion is the only way up the mountain reinforces the ego's need to be in control. Religion as a set of rules to follow has no connection to the heart. Religious dogma that stimulates fear by promising eternal punishment for unforgiven sin reinforces the ego's sense of threat.

The point is that true religion is about a heart overflowing with love. If one's beliefs are not working to scatter the smoke encasing the soul, it is time to rethink them. The sad history of the Christian church's failure to implement the vision of Jesus suggests that many Christians have some rethinking to do.

Finally, I would like to tell you a story that speaks to the relationship between religious experience and belief. I used this story in my novel, *Jeff's Journey*. It takes place forty years ago while our family was on sabbatical leave from my university in the mountains of North Carolina. I was supposed to be writing a book on US/Soviet Relations, but I never got to it. I spent the entire time reading and thinking about religion.

We had rented a small cabin located in a tiny village named Valle Crucis. The cabin was located 100 yards from the Watauga River. One morning in the fall, with the kids in school and Lyn at her new job helping a ski mountain prepare for the winter season, I was alone in the cabin reading. Around 9:30 two women knocked on the door, and I welcomed them in. Miranda and Edith were missionaries from a fundamentalist Baptist church about five miles from our cabin. We spent three hours together, and that visit began a relationship that lasted for a year. They came to visit every Wednesday, and I soon began attending their church from time to time.

The high point in our time together came on the second week in August when I attended a revival at their church. Revivals were scheduled for an entire week, but my lady friends requested I attend on Wednesday night which was "Bring a Guest Night."

I arrived at the church at 6:55 p.m. and hurried inside so as not to be late. I spotted the two couples immediately. They were seated in the middle of the church on the pulpit side. I squeezed in next to George, Edith's husband, fondly greeted both couples, and scanned the simply printed bulletin. From the look of things, it seemed that this would be nothing more than a traditional church service, and I was disappointed. I was expecting so much more from my first revival.

A hush came over the church members as the Reverend Belcher and a visiting minister entered from a side door, came to the middle of the church, and turned to face the congregation. The Reverend Belcher gave the invocation and introduced the first hymn. I had always been impressed with the volume of singing. Maybe it was the small size of the building, but in fact it was more than that. This congregation of 150 or so members could certainly belt out a hymn.

After the first hymn, there was a Scripture reading, a long, drawn-out prayer, an anthem by the choir, and the sermon. It took the sermon for me to realize that this service would be special after all. It was delivered by the visiting minister, the Reverend T. Sammy Paxton, who specialized in revivals. He toured a three-state area, visiting a different church each week.

T. Sammy looked as if I had cast him for the part. He was a sinister-looking man, thin as a snake, with a hawk-like nose. A fierce energy emanated from his face, causing me to wonder whether a smile would be able to erase his censorious demeanor. As he stood before the congregation, fire and brimstone raged from a raspy little voice that was at times so quiet I had to strain to hear, and then by the flip of a switch that voice began to rise until T. Sammy was actually shouting at his audience, toxic fumes spewing forth as he demanded that each member of the congregation admit their guilt and call on Jesus for forgiveness. Edith, along with several others in the congregation, was silently sobbing. As I surveyed the scene, the ones not crying seemed to be mesmerized. I saw no one who was asleep, bored, or otherwise distracted. Attentions were riveted. You couldn't avoid the glaring eyes. It was like traveling down a narrow highway and facing a car with its bright lights on. T. Sammy certainly held your attention. It was an impressive performance.

Following the sermon, the main show began as members of the congregation came up to the front of the church one at a time to make a testimonial. The first four or five confessed to some small transgression and then proclaimed Jesus had come into their lives to change their sinful ways and to make them into new people. I sat there intrigued, my analytical mind spinning in a judgmental fashion. T. Sammy had set the tone.

After these initial performances, a hush fell over the members for a second time. It was as if the entire congregation had been waiting for this moment. A man in his mid-twenties came forward. He was obviously nervous, and when he started speaking it was impossible to make out his words. At this point a young woman stepped forward to join him, looking more than a little pregnant and obviously the man's wife. The woman smiled up at her husband, took his hand, which calmed him down considerably, and gave him the confidence to begin his story again.

The congregation did not seem surprised by the story. He confessed to having an affair over the last six months which had abruptly ended when Jesus came into his life. The healing love of Jesus had saved the couple's marriage and changed the man into a new person. I sat there listening, admiring the man's courage, my judgmental mind softening as the drama unfolded.

What happened next was unbelievable. The whole congregation came up right then—the man had barely finished his story—to forgive the man and congratulate the couple. The service had no formal ending, that was it. There was a spontaneous outpouring of love and forgiveness for that young man which pervaded that tiny mountain Baptist church. You could feel its presence. It touched even the cynic from Massachusetts who had come to honor his two friends and to see a good show.

The ladies shoved me forward to meet the young couple.

"Lookey there," Miranda said as she poked me in the ribs. "There's his mother-in-law ahuggin' on him."

I was introduced to Kelley and Hal McLean, the young couple that had set off this spontaneous outpouring of compassion and forgiveness; Mrs. Eggers, the mother-in-law; the Reverend T. Sammy Paxton; as well as a host of friends of Miranda and Edith, some of whom I had seen before at previous services. I left the church at 9:45 p.m., after attending a reception of dessert and coffee in the church basement, feeling elated and strangely optimistic about life. I had even enjoyed my conversation at the reception with T. Sammy, discovering that he could in fact smile and that there was a pleasant person behind the harsh demeanor that had emanated from him during the sermon.

When I arrived back at the cabin, my family was sound asleep which turned out to be a blessing. It enabled me to get a glass of wine and sit on the porch overlooking the river to reflect on the experience. There was no question in my mind that God had been present at that church. The courageous couple standing before us, holding hands and asking for forgiveness, had touched me deeply, removing the smoke encasing my soul. Their performance obviously had a similar effect on many if not all of those in attendance. As I pointed out above, love was in the air. It was all around us. We could sense it, feel it. It was transforming, at least for me. My judgmental mindset left me and was replaced with a loving appreciation for these people.

However, as I sat there thinking about it, I was also convinced the encounter with God at the church had no relationship to the beliefs that most of those in attendance held. It in no way proved God was Jesus' father, that Jesus was God's only son, that Mary his mother was a virgin. In a similar way, the experience had nothing to say about whether Jesus physically rose from the dead, that Jesus as the Son of Man would return to rescue these

Christians and take them to heaven, that Jesus' death on the cross would save them from sin. There is in fact no relationship between religious experience and religious belief. An encounter with God fills your heart, but it has no content. It cannot be defined or rationally explained. In contrast, religious beliefs are human creations which often serve as impediments when it comes to encountering the divine.

4

A Religion of Compassion

IN THIS CHAPTER, WE examine the vision that emerges from the God-infused soul of the spiritual leaders we have profiled. We will begin with Jesus and examine his teachings by dividing them into three categories: the kingdom of God, the religion of Jesus, and the vision of Jesus. Our sources for this study will include the Sermon on the Mount in Matthew and Luke, and the parables which are found in the three Synoptic Gospels of Matthew, Mark, and Luke.

The primary focus of Jesus' ministry was the establishment of the kingdom of God. That was what he was sent to earth to do (Luke 4:42–43). This kingdom, as he tells us in the Lord's Prayer, will be a kingdom on earth patterned after God's kingdom in heaven (Matt 6:9–13; Luke 11:2–4).

Jesus gives no detailed description as to what this kingdom might look like. What he describes is not a place, but a state of affairs where God rules. In the parable of the secretly growing seed (Matt 4:26–29), Jesus makes clear that God will bring in this kingdom. The man in the parable scatters seed and then immediately falls asleep. Despite his lack of effort, the seed grows and the harvest comes. In all of Jesus' teachings on God's kingdom, no

Messiah is promised or even mentioned.[1] Jesus seems to oppose kingly rule. Only God can rule because rule by God will center on the power of love and not the tyrannical power of a king, which was the common situation in first-century Palestine.

Closely related to this idea, the kingdom of God will not be achieved through force. The parable of the sower makes that clear (Matt 13:1–9, 18–23; Mark 4:1–9, 13–20; Luke 8:4–9, 11–15). The farmer sows seed on paths, rocky soil, and among thorns which produce no crops. He also sows seed on good soil which leads to a plentiful harvest. As Jesus explains to his disciples, the seed represents the word of God. This word spreads peacefully. God conquerors through love, not force. The teachings on nonviolence in the Sermon on the Mount reinforce this point (Matt 5:21–22, 38–39).

What's this kingdom like? It's like yeast (Matt 13:33; Luke 13:20–21). It pervades life and gives it a new quality. This new quality comes from seeing the world with new eyes. As the famous parable of the mustard seed tells us (Matt 13:31–32; Mark 4:30–32; Luke 13:18–19) it begins on a very small scale. The mustard seed is one of the tiniest of all seeds and explodes forth in dramatic fashion.

Living in the kingdom produces a sense of profound joy. As Jesus tells us, it's like a man finding a treasure hidden in a field (Matt 13:44). He buries the treasure, and then he sells all he has so he can purchase the field. His ownership of the field and the treasure buried within it is a source of great joy. Living in a society organized around God's love is a cause for celebration.

A Jew is admitted into God's kingdom by living according to God's law, by doing God's will, by doing good works (Matt 7:21–22; Luke 6:45). You must place complete trust in God for this

1. Many Christians who are biblically literate might disagree with this statement, arguing that Jesus frequently promises the Son of Man will return to take them to heaven. I would argue, and many New Testament scholars agree, that the Son of Man statements in the Four Gospels come from the early church and not the historical Jesus. This is not the place for an elaborate defense of my position. The basic idea is that the statements of Jesus and those of the Son of Man are so different that the same person could not be making them. Note here that Jesus speaks of God's kingdom as coming to Israel while the Son of Man always refers to the kingdom in heaven. For a detailed discussion of this issue, see: Perrin, *Rediscovering the Teachings of Jesus.*

miracle to come about (Matt 6:25–34; Luke 12:22–32). It must be your central focus (Matt 8:21–22; 16:24–25).

Moving to the religion of Jesus, you can't read the Sermon on the Mount without concluding that Jesus was a loyal Jew. He firmly believed in the necessity of obeying God's law; however, many of his reforms were seen as radical by the Jewish religious establishment. He overturns Moses on divorce and challenges the temple cult which was based on atoning sacrifice. His kingdom was for the poor, the sinners, those who were considered outsiders, the hated tax collectors, and the people Jewish law defined as unrighteous. He saw purity rules as unimportant and called on his people to focus on the weightier parts of the law like economic and social justice. Why this focus? Simply because God is inclusive. All members of society would be equal in God's kingdom, a radical idea for first-century Palestine. Jesus came to this conclusion because he possessed a heart that was overflowing with God's love.

While remaining within the broader outlook of Jewish tradition, he had a unique perspective on religion. His God was one of love and forgiveness. He addressed God as *abba*, a term of endearment.[2] In the well-known parable of the prodigal son (Luke 15:11–32), the younger of two sons claims his inheritance, seeks his fortune, and blows it. He ends up working on a pig farm, an abomination for a Jew, and concludes that his father's servants are better off than he is. He returns home, begging to be one of those servants; but to his great surprise his father welcomes him with open arms and orders a celebration. The father in the parable is seen as God, and the point is that this is a God who loves and forgives. Compassion is God's most important attribute, a love that moves away from self to take care of the needs of others.

It is interesting to contrast Jesus' God of love and compassion with the gods of the Roman Empire in the first century. The Roman Empire was a polytheistic civilization with people worshipping several gods and goddesses. These deities were responsible for overseeing specific aspects of life. They helped to shape the lives of people on a daily basis.

2. Cobb, *Jesus' Abba.*

The gods of the Roman Empire were honored in temples with elaborate rituals and festivals. Any favorable outcome in their particular realm was attributed to them. An unfavorable outcome was seen as an expression of their anger. These gods had no interest in morality. Their chief concern was for people to honor them through specific rituals and the proper amount of tribute. They were moody and capricious. Proper worship was seen as the key to appeasing their wrath. These gods were from a different planet than the God of love and compassion espoused by Jesus.

The parable of the Pharisee and the tax collector (Luke 18:9–14) provides an important insight into the workings of the divine/human relationship. Both go to the temple to pray. The Pharisee tells God how good he is. His attitude is self-righteous, proud, and egodriven. The tax collector humbly asks God for forgiveness because he is a sinner. Jesus praises the tax collector. As was pointed out in chapter 3, an egodriven, self-righteous perspective prevents you from encountering the love of God emanating from your soul. The self-righteous, egodriven perspective of the older son in the parable of the prodigal son makes the same point.

Finally, the good Samaritan (Luke 10:30–36) tells us that the religion of Jesus is not about ritual or belief, but rather about following the dictates of your heart. A man on a trip from Jerusalem to Jericho was accosted by bandits and left on the side of the road half dead. A priest and a Levite, representing the religious establishment centered around the temple, saw the man suffering on the side of the road and passed him by. Sadly, they practiced a religion based on ritual and belief and consequently were unable to experience the deep love of God which would have led them to reach out to the victim.

In contrast, a Samaritan from a group of people hated by Palestinian Jews was moved by compassion. He took care of the man, bandaging his wounds and putting him up at an inn so he could recover. "Moved with compassion" (v. 33) is the key phrase. The Samaritan followed the dictates of his heart. That is where the truth of religion lies.

The parable of the sheep and the goats (Matt 25:31–46) makes the same point. In this case, people are judged not in terms of whether they believe in Jesus, but rather in terms of whether they served their neighbor. Did their hearts go out to those who are poor, hungry, thirsty, lacking clothes, or to a stranger in need of companionship?

In Matthew 23 and Luke 11 Jesus makes a sevenfold indictment of the scribes and Pharisees. The essence of his attack is that they ignore the weightier matters of the law—justice, mercy, and good faith (Matt 23:23; Luke 11:42). The Pharisees are all about appearance, looking good, and petty matters within the law like washing before a meal and scrupulously honoring the sabbath by refraining from work.

Economic justice is a major focus of Jesus' teachings. In the Lord's Prayer he urges people to forgive those who are in debt to them (Matt 6:12). He tells his followers that one cannot become a disciple unless he renounces his wealth (Luke 14:33). He tells the rich man that before he can enter God's kingdom he must sell his possessions and give the money to the poor (Matt 19:16–22). God's kingdom is for the poor, the disadvantaged, the ignored, the widows, and the orphans. It is a place where the last will be first. You can't serve two masters: God and the world (Matt 6:25; Luke 6:13).

It is also informative to look at the first Christian community under Jesus' brother James in Jerusalem. This community, inspired by the teachings of Jesus, was based on neighbor need and the sharing of wealth. Private property was given to the poor and what remained was shared equally:

> And all who shared the faith owned everything in common; they sold their goods and possessions and distributed the proceeds among themselves according to what each one needed. (Acts 2:44–45; see also 4:32–35)

As I pointed out above, the kingdom will be brought in peacefully. Love and generosity will replace retaliation (Matt 5:38–42; Luke 6:29–30). Jesus taught his followers to love their enemies and to pray for those who persecuted them (Matt 5:43–48). Jesus counseled his listeners at the Sermon on the Mount to offer no resistance to the wicked. If anyone hits you on the right cheek, offer him the other cheek as well (Matt 5:39–40).

Jesus loved to celebrate with meals, and he was always inclusive. His table included tax collectors, lepers, women, and all those who were isolated socially and in need of companionship. In the parable of the laborers at the vineyard (Matt 20:1–11), all the day laborers were paid the same wage even though they worked a different number of hours. There is a strong hint that the hiring landlord is God and the vineyard is Israel. The idea that drives the parable is the radical equality that characterized God's kingdom.

As with religion, the key to ethics is inner disposition or the health of the human heart. Yes, you should not kill, but anyone who is angry at his brother is just as guilty. Yes, you must not commit adultery, but if a man looks at a woman with lust you are committing adultery in your heart (Matt 5:21–28). A heart that overflows with love will serve his neighbor, take care of widows, share his wealth, and refrain from lashing out with violence. Such a stance describes a religion in which the God of love and compassion is well known.

Christians have criticized Jesus' teachings for being impractical. Others have argued they are an interim ethic, a way of living until the kingdom of God comes with power at the end of time, but not a civilization ethic, a set of teachings with relevance 2,000 years later.

For me, these criticisms miss the point. I see Jesus' teachings as revelation. He is telling us what God's kingdom will look like. His vision is based on what would happen when God's love infuses real-life situations, when God's love is used to organize society. He is providing us with a vision of what the world might look like if we lived from the center of our souls.

Beautiful fruits result from personal transformation as we see with the apostle Paul. When you center your life in God as seen in Jesus, the old self dies and a new one is born. You see the world differently. The mind is transformed in such a way as to enable you to carry out the vision of God (Rom 12:2).

Paul sees himself as a Jew (see Rom 9–11) and never intends to start a new religion. His vision is remarkably similar to that of Jesus. His statement on inclusion is one of the most beautiful passages in religious literature. We forget that he was a first-century man:

> There can be neither Jew nor Greek, there can be neither slave nor freeman, there can be neither male nor female—for you are all one in Christ. (Gal 3:28)

He exhorts us to never pay back evil with evil, to be at peace with everyone, and to not seek revenge. If your enemy is hungry, give him something to eat (Rom 12:17–20). Like Jesus, he calls on us to love our neighbor as ourselves. This is the essence of the law (Rom 13:11). He has a long section in Romans urging people to build each other up rather than tear each other down (14:1–21). We must look for the good in others (Rom 15:1). Finally, he urges his followers in Corinth to give generously to the poor (2 Cor 9:6–13).

With regard to the prophets, Amos, the earliest of the Old Testament prophets, received his call to serve God in 750 BCE while he was attending his flock. He lived at a time of peace and prosperity which was characterized by huge discrepancies in wealth and shallow, insincere worship. Here is his answer to these problems—one of my favorites:

> I hate, I scorn your festivals, I take no pleasure in your solemn assemblies. When you bring me burnt offerings, your oblations, I do not accept them, and I do not look at your communion sacrifices of fat cattle. Spare me the din of your chanting, let me hear none of your strumming on lyres, but let justice flow like water, and uprightness like a never-failing stream. (Amos 5:21–24)

For Amos, religion was not about ritual and belief, but rather about translating the deep love he sensed in his heart to solve the problems of economic and social justice.

Isaiah was called at about the same time, and thus he spoke to similar problems. He lashes out at the superficiality of worship at the temple. God was sick of the endless sacrifices (Isa 1:11–13). Instead, he urged the people of Israel to:

> Cease doing evil. Learn to do good, search for justice,
> discipline the violent, be just to the orphan, plead for the
> widow. (1:16–17)

In addition, he has a vision of universal peace that will take place in the final days.

> Then he will judge between the nations and arbitrate
> between many peoples. They will hammer their swords
> into plowshares and their spears into sickles. Nation will
> not lift sword against nation, no longer will they learn
> how to make war. (2:4)

Jeremiah arrived on the scene more than a hundred years later. He was the prophet of Judah's decline and fall under colonial rule. His call came in 627 BCE. He is the prophet of forgiveness and God's love. Religion is a matter of the heart. The heart is the meeting place for God and man. Because Israel had sinned, the old covenant was annulled and replaced with a new covenant based on circumcision of the heart. The new covenant would no longer be based on tablets of stone, but rather an inward sense of God's love. Then the people of Israel would know Yahweh (Jer 31:33–34). Jeremiah was also concerned with insincere worship (see ch. 7), and the needs of the poor (22:13–17).

Ezekiel was a strange one. He was a priest who was part of the exile in Babylon in 597 BCE. As a priest he was interested in the inner meaning of ritual, a form of ritual that enlarged the heart. He had a keen sense of God's world becoming manifest in everyday life. His vision experiences (chs. 8–11) taught him that God was deep love and essential mystery. He prophesied that God would bring his people out of exile; and, like Jeremiah, God would give the people a new covenant written on their hearts so that they could finally obey. Ethical living was not seen as obeying religious law, but rather it came from a transformed heart. When Israel returned from their captivity in Babylon, Ezekiel envisioned God as saying:

> I shall give them a single heart and shall put a new spirit
> in them; I shall remove the heart of stone from their
> bodies and give them a heart of flesh, so that they can

keep my laws, respect my judgments and put them into
practice. (11:19–20)

Finally, with regard to myself, I have changed from coming
to know God in two important ways. First, at a personal level, I
am far more at peace with myself than I was twenty-five years ago
when I began the inner work described in the previous chapter.
The change has not been dramatic and earth-shaking as the example of Paul suggests, but over the twenty-five years of this journey
the change has been significant as I have come to recognize the
source of my insecurities and rejected them.

I now do my work as a writer because it is fun, a wonderful
way to spend four or five hours a day in retirement, and not out
of some need and all-consuming drive to impress others. I have
become far more able to see the humanity of people I disagree with
politically. I have learned how to listen, to surrender control, and
to judge others less. I think some of my friends have come to think
I live in La La land. While that may be true, it is a real blessing to
get up each morning and see the world as beautiful and good.

With regard to my lifelong goal to live according to the teachings of Jesus, it has been helpful to come to a better understanding
of how God works in the world. Four or five years ago I spoke at
length with a woman who worked for the Stacey Abrams Founda-
tion in Atlanta to increase voter registration in Georgia. Here is
one example of what I learned that night. My friend told me about
a retired school teacher who had voted for thirty years at her old
school which was no more than a ten-minute walk from her house.
The wait time for voting was less than fifteen minutes. Because
of changes made in the law by the Republican legislature, her old
precinct was closed. She now has to vote at a high school on the
other side of Atlanta which requires a forty-five minute bus ride
and a three- or four-hour wait.

Close your eyes for a minute and think about this retired Af-
rican American schoolteacher. If the thought floats through your
awareness that this is unfair and a reform of the law needs to be
made, that thought, according to process theology, comes from
God. I am a big fan of the theology developed by Alfred North

Whitehead, Charles Hartshorne, and John Cobb because it so accurately explains my experience.[3]

According to process theological thinking, humans are decisionmakers. We make decisions based on several factors—past experiences, our needs and demands of the moment, and a sense of love and goodness that floats through our awareness. That vision of love and goodness comes from God. God lures us to decide for the best interest of others, but God never coerces. Humans remain free to choose how they will respond to a particular event or demand in their life.

Think about a second-grader, a little African-American girl who smiles at you with two missing front teeth. You meet her in a chaotic classroom with thirty-five other students and a substitute teacher. There are armed guards at the entrance to the school, and the plaster in the hall leading to her classroom is falling from the ceiling. What thoughts are going through your mind?

I taught political science at the college level for twenty years. Put yourself for a brief moment in my classroom for a course on American foreign policy. The topic for the day is NATO policy for containing the Soviet Union. I tell you, and you are writing this down furiously, that tactical nuclear weapons are in the hands of American field commanders to be used to counter a Soviet invasion of Germany. These weapons have been deployed to save money. Countering the Soviet threat with an equivalent conventional force has been deemed to be too expensive. I also tell you that the collateral damage to civilians from our using tactical nuclear weapons, bombs three to five times as powerful as the ones that fell on Hiroshima and Nagasaki at the end of World War II, would be horrific.

Assuming you have not fallen asleep, what thoughts are floating through your awareness? If you are thinking there must be a better way, that thought most likely comes from God. God is gently urging you to become involved in politics. You say to yourself, well I better not participate in a protest on this issue because I'm not well-informed on national security issues. Think again. This is

3. Whitehead, *Process and Reality*; Hartshorne, *Natural Theology for Our Time*; and Cobb, *Christian Natural Theology*.

God speaking. If you decide to act politically, you will be working with God to make the world a better place.

Here's the point of all this. To work with God to make the world a better place, you must hear God's voice among competing voices that are often loud and insistent. Clearing the smoke surrounding my soul has made hearing the voice of God so much easier.

The above represents a brief overview of the ethical visions of the spiritual leaders I have profiled. In each case, God was all about love and compassion. Deep encounters of divine love transformed them. With their souls leading the way, they presented a vision of religion that was inclusive, with a passion for economic and social justice. Religion was not about ritual or belief, but rather what was crucial was the health of your heart. It was all about knowing God in a deep, experiential sense and living from the center of your soul. When that happens, good fruit is produced. You join with God to make the world a better place.

I can think of no higher calling, and this is not about utopian nonsense. Tibetan Buddhism proved such an approach to spiritual growth can work. It reconstructed Tibet from a warlike kingdom into a loving theocracy by transforming people. Monks replaced soldiers. These monks provided a bureaucracy to manage the daily affairs of the society based on the practice of love and compassion.

While China has tried to destroy this culture, it has demonstrated remarkable resiliency. When Lyn and I were there eight years ago, I asked our Tibetan guide about this question. He assured me the Dalai Lama was still worshipped by the vast majority of the people and that despite the setbacks delivered by China the people still believed the practice of compassion and nonviolence was the best approach.

Obviously, the United States could not be ruled by a Tibetan-style theocracy, but the spiritual growth of our citizens would make politics look a lot different from the hyperpartisan brawl now being practiced. It would also make possible the solution to problems of economic and social justice, gun violence, climate change, and the possession of nuclear weapons—all of which threaten our society and the world in significant ways.

5

Conclusion

FOR MOST CHRISTIANS THE focus of their religion is the attainment of salvation in heaven. To live forever: what a nice thought! It has been the driving force behind the growth of Christianity for 2,000 years.

There are several problems with this focus for Christianity. As I point out in the first chapter, there is much confusion in the New Testament over what salvation is all about. Is it for Israel or the whole world? Will it take place in heaven or on earth? Do you earn your way to heaven or does it come as a gift from God? Was the resurrection of Jesus a physical event or a vision experience? Where is heaven for that matter? Evangelicals believe it is up there in the sky, which is difficult to imagine when you acknowledge the fact that the earth is a spherical globe. Where is up there with such a body? Why has the second coming of Jesus been so long in coming? The New Testament promised Jesus' return was imminent, within the first century.

With problems such as these, the view of many Christians that the Bible is the literal word of God is indefensible. It also suggests that the prospect of salvation in heaven is the product of wishful thinking. The idea of eternal life with God in heaven is an amazing prospect. For such a promise to be credible, it must have strong evidence to support it. As the analysis in chapter 1 indicates, one cannot rely on the evidence in the New Testament to provide that credibility.

In addition to the questions above, there are historical problems surrounding the question of salvation that need to be considered. The idea for salvation has Jewish roots. When Moses led his people out of Egypt as described in the book of Exodus, he and God made a covenant on Mount Sinai. In the covenant, God promised to protect Israel in return for Jews obeying God's law. This agreement seemed to work out well for a long time. Israel flourished under God's protection during the reigns of Kings David and Solomon.

Things started falling apart after Solomon's death around 1,000 BCE. Israel split into a Northern and Southern Kingdom. This weakened state allowed Assyria to conquer the Northern Kingdom in 722 BCE. Babylon captured Judah, the Southern Kingdom, 200 years later. As a result, Israel became a colonized nation.

How could this happen? The covenant said that God was supposed to protect Israel. The prophets answered this question by saying that God was no longer protecting Israel because Israel had sinned. Israel was therefore responsible for breaking the covenant, not God. The message of the prophets was not only about punishment, however. Their collective anger over Israel's sin was always tempered by hope. That hope was the salvation of Israel as a nation. The idea was that God would honor his covenant by sending a Messiah to rescue Israel. This Messiah, in the person of a king or a great military leader, would restore Israel's glory as a nation. This Messiah would establish God's kingdom on earth.

The prophetic answer worked for many years until the second century BCE. At that time Israel was under Syrian colonial rule. In 175 BCE, a nasty Syrian king named Antiochus IV Epiphanes came into power with the goal of increasing his country's control over Israel. He set out to destroy Judaism as a religion. He ordered icons of Greek gods to be installed in the temple at Jerusalem; pigs, an animal that is anathema to Jews, were sacrificed on the temple altar; and he began executing Jews for circumcising their children. Jews were now being punished for obeying God's law. The answer from the prophets no longer worked.

Into this void of meaning and despair the prophet Daniel came to the rescue. Daniel argued that Israel's misery was not the result of divine punishment, but rather the actions of Satan, the power of evil. This Satan was out to control the world. God, however, would honor the covenant. There would soon come an end time, a time that was so bad God would intervene to rescue the righteous among the people of Israel. God would do that by sending his divine agent, the Son of Man, from the clouds of heaven to judge the people of Israel and rescue the righteous by taking them to heaven. The expectation of the time when these events would take place was imminent, within the first century.

A central part of this history was the covenant God made with Israel. Does God make binding legal agreements with people? Would a God of love specifically select one nation to favor and protect? There is also a big problem with the Daniel prophecy which provides the basis for the Christian belief in the second coming. Unfortunately, the book of Daniel does not reflect the word of God, but is rather a fraudulent work.

Here's the problem. Daniel claims to be a prophet of the sixth century BCE (Dan 1:1–8). He makes predictions relating to events in the second century (ch. 11). The problem is that there is a vast consensus among biblical scholars that the book of Daniel was actually written in the second century BCE. My Bible, the Jerusalem Bible, a product of the Roman Catholic Church, has a brief introduction to Daniel which claims the book was written between 167 and 164 BCE.

The author of Daniel lied about when he wrote the book to enhance his credibility as a prophet. He looks really good. What he writes about in the second century, happened. The problem is that the author of Daniel was not predicting the future; but writing history, and thus deceiving people with his prophetic claims.

The arguments presented above lead me to conclude the Christian salvation myth is not well supported. In making this claim, I don't aim to deny the possibility of life after death. Many spiritual traditions adopt such a belief in one form or another. The literature on near-death experiences, while controversial, is quite amazing.[1] Life is constantly renewing itself. What I'm suggesting is the Christian version of that belief is not very convincing. What happens when life ends remains a mystery which will stay with us forever. As a result, the central thesis of this book is that we focus religion on life on earth, on what we know to be real and not something based on fanciful thinking. It is interesting that this approach to religion was the one advocated by Jesus. His central concern was to bring God's rule, the rule of love and kindness, to Israel.

I have a good friend who knows my theological positions quite well. He once told me: "Rick, leave conservative Christians alone. If they want to live in salvation La La land, let them. Everyone needs a Santa Claus. What harm will it do?"

Another good friend, Diane Dreher, has written a wonderful book entitled *The Tao of Inner Peace* which answers that question. She describes a society where many people are anxious, angry, depressed, and mentally exhausted. Because the mass media bombards us with a steady diet of violence, many live in chronic fear of being attacked. In a culture that champions competition and winning at any price, people have lost trust in one another. Excessive consumption results from an attempt to fill an inner emptiness. Her analysis echoes that of the Dalai Lama, who has long argued that modern life in the developed world is full of anxiety, addiction, isolation, depression, worry, and mental exhaustion.

A Christian focus on knowing God in a deep experiential sense heals those problems. Look at the life of Paul. The discovery of a God of love residing in his soul transformed him from a mean-spirited, petty man into a loving servant. Carl Jung, one of the most renowned psychotherapists of the twentieth century,

---

1. Readers interested in getting started on this topic can consult: Moody, *Life After Life*; Newton, *Journey of Souls*; Alexander, *Proof of Heaven*; and Long, *Evidence of the Afterlife*.

proclaimed the key to his work was not the treatment of psychological problems, but rather in helping his patients to know God in a deep, experiential way.[2]

In addition, as the ethical profiles in chapter 4 suggest, a changed focus in our religion will go a long way toward solving some very dangerous problems. Climate change is already changing the world in profoundly negative ways. It's a Christian problem because it's caused by excessive greed and consumption which runs contrary to the focus on simple living advocated by Jesus. If not brought under control, our precious planet will be threatened with destruction. Conservative Christians will finally have their end times.

Nuclear weapons pose a similar long-term threat. Economic inequality is exploding both here and around the globe. Racial injustice is also a problem here and abroad. Our democracy is threatened by extreme polarization, the lack of civility among politicians, and a wing of the Republican party bent on decreasing voter turnout among people of color. Most of these politicians claim to be Christian. They profess to believe in God, which I'm sure they do. Sadly, their behavior tells me they don't know God very well.

What would a changed focus look like? Jesus would become what he most likely was—an inspired teacher and a wonderful human being. Christians would spend less time studying the Bible and more time in nature. We need to consider a new master story to replace the two creation stories in Genesis. Such a story should connect all people together, provide meaning, and point to God by creating a sense of awe and wonder. I nominate *The Universe Story* as described in the wonderful book by Brian Swimme and Thomas Berry under that title.[3] This story examines the unfolding of the universe from the big bang to the present. It leaves the reader with a deep sense of awe and worder, which removes the smoke allowing goodness and love to take over one's personality.

Salvation would be redefined away from concern over sin and eternal life in heaven to the need to heal both individuals and the planet. New songs with lyrics reflecting postmodern society

2. Jung, *Memories, Dreams, Reflections.*
3. Swimme and Berry, *Universe Story.*

need to be introduced. Churches would place a much greater emphasis on healing the egos of their members and on teaching them Eastern spiritual techniques which have helped people come to know God for centuries. Spiritual leaders would inspire their congregants with profiles of the thousands of mystics both within the Christian tradition and beyond it. The point is: you can do it too. Bringing all this together, the focus of worship would be on getting to know God in a deep, experiential sense. The exact form of the liturgy would differ for each congregation. The only test would be: Does it bring God's presence alive? For those interested in exploring new forms of liturgy, check out the "Plan Your Service" section of the ProgressiveChristianity.org website.

A change in focus from biblical belief and salvation in heaven to getting to know God in a deep, experiential way would not only help individuals and the planet heal, but it would also save our religion. Christianity in the postmodern world is experiencing a dramatic decline. When Lyn and I travel to Western Europe, the churches we come across have become museums. Active church membership as defined by attending religious services at least once a month has declined in Western Europe to 22 percent.[4]

This decline has also come to America. A recent poll from the Pew Research Center (12/20/21) indicates that while 75 percent of Americans declared themselves to be Christian ten years ago, that number is only 63 percent today.[5] If this trend continues, Christians will make up less than half of the population in a few decades.[6]

There are many reasons for this decline. An important one is the problems discussed in chapter 1. Christian doctrine is no longer credible because of all the confusion found in the New Testament. A related problem is modern science. Developments in modern science have been devastating to a literal reading of the Bible. The miracle stories no longer make sense. A virgin birth is

4. Tornielli, "Statistics on the Slow Evaporation of European Christianity," para. 2.

5. Schaeffer, "Striking Findings for 2021," poll 9.

6. "Modeling the Future of Religion in America," para. 1.

hard to imagine. Where did Jesus go when he ascended to heaven? Where is heaven anyway?

In addition, modern life has taken us out of God's world. People in the postmodern West live in a world mostly of their own creation. Our houses shield us from nature and isolate us from our neighbors. Our electronic devices consume more and more of our time and function to create a world of virtual reality—a decidedly human creation. For thousands of years people experienced nature in a deep way as an everyday occurrence. Today such encounters have been relegated to an occasional outing. A deep experience of the beauty and wonder of nature creates a sense of awe and mystery. Awe and wonder shock us out of a mindset defined by narrow, self-centered interests, which clears the smoke from our soul.

The one thing that hasn't changed in the last 2,000 years is God. When your heart is overflowing with love, belief is no longer relevant. You could care less about the confusion surrounding beliefs within the New Testament. A full heart that results from meeting God has nothing to do with science. The two perspectives, religion and science, can exist comfortably together. By its very nature belief separates, it divides. A full heart tells us all is one. Finally, belief as I understand it means a proposition that can't be proven. As a result, it's time to move beyond it. Recreating the Christian religion around a positive program of getting to know God will attract the growing number of people who have left the institutional church but answer survey data by checking the "Spiritual" box.

Though most people will settle for lives of conformity and safe passage, it's time to get both honest and real with ourselves. A religion of belief is a human creation which, as the Buddha teaches, only gets in the way of our understanding the truth about God. A Christianity of belief has not helped to heal the many problems the world has faced over the last 2,000 years, but has sadly often made the problems worse. For the first time the fate of the world is in our hands. What will we do about this terrifying responsibility? We must change in order to save God's world and our precious planet. A God of love is waiting for us to clear away the smoke surrounding our souls. It's time for us to get to know this loving presence that can transform our lives and heal the many dangerous problems that confront us.

Bibliography

Alexander, Eben. *Proof of Heaven*. New York: Simon & Schuster, 2012.

Allison, Dale C., Jr. *The Historical Christ and the Theological Jesus*. Grand Rapids: Eerdmans, 2009.

Anderson, Paul N. *The Riddles of the Fourth Gospel*. Minneapolis: Fortress, 2011.

Armstrong, Karen. *St. Paul: The Apostle We Love to Hate*. New York: Amazon, 2015.

Borg, Marcus J. *Meeting Jesus Again for the First Time*. San Francisco: HarperOne, 2009.

Borg, Marcus J., and John Dominic Crossan. *The First Paul*. New York: HarperCollins, 2009.

Brueggemann, Walter. *The Prophetic Imagination*. Minneapolis: Fortress, 2018.

Buber, Martin. *I and Thou*. New York: Scribner, 1970.

Burklo, Jim. *Mindful Christianity*. Haworth, NJ: St. Johann, 2017.

Bushby, Joshua. "Why Climate Change Matters More Than Anything Else." *Foreign Affairs* 97.4 (July-August 2018) 49–57.

Carroll, James. *Constantine's Sword*. New York: Houghton Mifflin, 2001.

Cobb, John B., Jr., *A Christian Natural Theology*. Second Edition. Louisville: Westminister John Knox, 2007.

———. *Jesus' Abba: The God Who Has Not Failed*. Minneapolis: Fortress, 2016.

Corbett, Lionel. *The Religious Function of the Psyche*. New York: Routledge, 1988.

Crossan, John Dominic. *The Historical Jesus*. San Francisco: HarperCollins, 1992.

Bibliography

Ehrman, Bart D. *Jesus: Apocalyptic Prophet for the New Millennium*. New York: Oxford University Press, 1999.

Ellsberg, Daniel. *The Doomsday Machine*. New York: Bloomsbury, 2017.

Flannery, Francis, and Rodney A. Werline, eds. *The Bible in Political Debate*. New York: Bloombury, 2012.

Fox, Matthew. *Christian Mystics*. Novato, CA: New World Library, 2011.

———. *One River, Many Wells*. New York: Tarcher, 2004.

Frantz, Jeffrey E. *The God You Didn't Know You Could Believe In*. Haworth, NJ: St. Johann, 2020.

Fredriksen, Paula. *Jesus of Nazareth: King of the Jews*. New York: Knopf, 1999.

Hartshorne, Charles. *Natural Theology for Our Time*. Second Edition. Louisville: Westminister John Knox, 2077.

Herrick, Rick. *The Case against Evangelical Christianity*. Second Edition. Cambridge, MA: Charles River, 2011.

History.com Editors. "Rwandan Genocide." *History.com*, October 14, 2009. https://www.history.com/topics/africa/rwandan genocide.

Jenkins, Philip. *Jesus Wars*. San Francisco: HarperCollins, 2010.

Jung, Carl Gustav. *Memories, Dreams, Reflections*. New York: Vintage, 2011.

Long, Jeffrey. *Evidence of the Afterlife*. San Francisco: HarperOne, 2010.

MacCulloch, Diarmaid. *Christianity: The First Three Thousand Years*. New York: Viking, 2009.

Metaxas, Eric. *Bonhoeffer: Pastor, Martyr, Prophet, Spy*. Nashville: Nelson, 2010.

"Modeling the Future of Religion in America." *Pew Research Center*, September 13, 2022. https://www.pewresearch.org/religion/2022/09/13/modeling-the-future-of-religion-in-america/.

Moody, Raymond A., Jr. *Life After Life*. San Francisco: HarperOne, 2015.

Naranjo, Claudio, and Robert E. Ornstein. *On the Psychology of Meditation*. New York: Viking, 1971.

Newton, Michael B. *Journey of Souls*. Woodbury, MN: Llewellyn, 1994.

Perrin, Norman. *Rediscovering the Teachings of Jesus*. New York: Harper & Row, 1976.

Rohr, Richard. *What the Mystics Know*. Dallas: Crossroads, 2019.

Schaeffer, Katherine. "Striking Findings for 2021." *Pew Research Center*, December 17, 2021. https://www.pewresearch.org/fact-tank/2021/12/17/striking-findings-from-2021/.

Swimme, Brian, and Thomas Berry. *The Universe Story*. San Francisco: HarperOne, 1994.

Thames, Knox. "Putin Is After More than Land—He Wants the Religious Soul of Ukraine." *Religion News Service*, February 24, 2022. https://religionnews.com/2022/02/24/putin-is-after-more-than-land-he-wants-the-religious-soul-of-ukraine/.

Tornielli, Andrea. "The Statistics on the Slow Evaporation of European Christianity." *Mercator.net*, May 30, 2018. https://mercatornet.com/the-statistics-on-the-slow-evaporation-of-european-christianity/23242/.

Underhill, Evelyn. *Practical Mysticism*. New York: Digireads.com, 2010.

Bibliography

Van Biema, David, and Jeff Chu. "Does God Want You To Be Rich?" *Time Magazine*, September 10, 2006. https://content.time.com/time/magazine/article/0,9171,1533448-2,00.html

Whitehead, Alfred North. *Process and Reality: An Essay in Cosmology.* New York: Macmillan, 1929.

Made in the USA
Monee, IL
15 January 2023